Writing Habit

Mastery

How to Write 2,000 Words a Day and Forever Cure Writer's Block

By S.J. Scott

http://www.HabitBooks.com

January 2014
Copyright © 2014 S.J. Scott
All rights reserved worldwide.

Published by Archangel Ink

ISBN 1495473600
ISBN-13: 978-1495473609

Disclaimer

No part of this publication may be reproduced or transmitted in any form or by any means, mechanical or electronic, including photocopying or recording, or by any information storage and retrieval system, or transmitted by email without permission in writing from the publisher.

While all attempts have been made to verify the information provided in this publication, neither the author nor the publisher assumes any responsibility for errors, omissions, or contrary interpretations of the subject matter herein.

This book is for entertainment purposes only. The views expressed are those of the author alone, and should not be taken as expert instruction or commands. The reader is responsible for his or her own actions.

Adherence to all applicable laws and regulations, including international, federal, state, and local governing professional licensing, business practices, advertising, and all other aspects of doing business in the US, Canada, or any other jurisdiction is the sole responsibility of the purchaser or reader.

Neither the author nor the publisher assumes any responsibility or liability whatsoever on the behalf of the purchaser or reader of these materials.

Any perceived slight of any individual or organization is purely unintentional.

Table of Contents

Introduction

Have you always wanted to write a novel, but never seem able to get past the first few chapters? Do you have an eBook rattling around in your brain, but just can't get it down on paper? Do you get stuck with writer's block when you finally do sit down in front of the computer?

This book will teach you how to:

• Learn specific routines that will help you develop a long-term writing habit.

• Overcome writer's block so you will know what you want to write every single time you settle in to write.

• Write fast by following a specific process for creating content.

It's frustrating to have an idea for a great book but never seem to be able to find time to actually write it.

I also know you're busy. You've got a zillion things running through your head. Work, kids, relationships, home projects—it seems like there's never a perfect time to write your book or screenplay. Even when you do sit down to work on your writing project, you've let so much time lapse in between that you've forgotten what you've completed and what needs to be done next.

The truth is this: Successful writers don't have more time than you do.

They *make* time to write.

Not only do they make time, but they have also figured out writing routines that help them avoid writer's block altogether.

This book is designed to help you figure out how to do exactly that, while working with your schedule and constraints.

What you *need* are tools that will help you develop a sustainable writing habit and demolish writer's block. It took me a great deal of time, research, and perfecting of the process to develop a writing habit that works every day.

Who Am I?

My name is S.J. Scott. I run the blog Develop Good Habits (http://www.developgoodhabits.com). The goal of my site is to show how *continuous* habit development can lead to a better life. Instead of lecturing you, I provide simple strategies that can be easily added to any busy life. It's been my experience that the best way to make a lasting change is to develop a single quality habit at a time.

One habit that challenged me for many years was *writing*. I struggled with it on a daily basis and often encountered writer's block. But everything changed when I adapted a strategic mindset. Now, I consistently write between 60,000 to 75,000 words a month, which has helped me create 600+ blog posts and 35 Kindle books in the last few years. All of this is due to having the confidence to sit down every day and crank out a few thousand words.

Why Write 2,000 Words a Day?

One of the key factors to effectively developing a new habit is choosing a specific, measurable goal. For example, if someone wants to develop a running habit, they will be more likely to be successful if they commit to jogging for 15 minutes each day than if they pledge to "run more often."

By committing to writing a **set number of words per day**, you will succeed.

This works because:

• You can accomplish small daily goals much more easily than huge long-term goals.

• It's not intimidating to sit down to write 2,000 words, but it's difficult to set aside a week to do nothing but write.

• Hitting that word count goal will turn into a daily writing habit that carries far beyond a single project.

I chose the goal of 2,000 words a day because that's what I've found to be most effective for me. (Actually, I normally write 2,700 words a day. Since I take weekends off, this averages out to 2,000 words each day.)

If you write 2,000 words each day, you will:

- Write 14,000 words per week.
- Complete a small eBook in three to four weeks.
- Finish a first draft of an average novel in two months.
- Publish one *quality* blog post every day.

I realize you may not write at the same pace that I do. You might only be able to write 500 or 1,000 words a day. Or, you might have more time than I do (or write faster than I do) and choose to write 3,000 or 10,000 words each day. The important thing is to establish a daily word count goal and then stick to it.

How to Overcome Writer's Block with a Writing Habit

Most people don't write because of a creative form of procrastination. Often it's due to an uncertainty of what to say. Perhaps they have gotten stuck in the past. Or maybe they don't understand the power of smart outlining. Or they might think it's easier to *daydream* about a book instead of taking action.

No matter *what* the reason, you'll discover it's easy to overcome writer's block if you turn writing into a habit. Instead of *guessing* what you'll create each day, you'll learn how to map out your ideas and turn your thoughts into quality content.

Unlike a lot of popular writing books that talk about the glory of writing, this book is highly actionable. You will learn a practical writing process that *actually* works. My goal is to help you develop a writing habit that results in a finished book, completed blog posts or a polished screenplay.

Ready to get started?

Then let's get to it.

The Psychology of the Daily Writing Habit

You might find it an odd concept to consider developing a writing "habit." After all, many of us think of habits as bad things we wish we'd stop doing, like biting our nails or staying up too late. Fortunately, good habits can lead to rewarding improvements in our lives.

Habits are powerful because they become second nature. If you develop a habit of stretching soon after you wake up, you will find yourself rolling right into that yoga pose—and enjoying it. If you develop the habit of drinking water throughout the day, soda will lose its appeal and you'll find yourself longing for a tall cold glass of H2O.

Once you've established writing habits, you'll find yourself avoiding old bad habits, like succumbing to writer's block.

Think of it this way:

Let's say you run the same route every day. On this route is a pothole, right in the middle of your path. A smart runner will plan a running route that swerves around the pothole, right? You might trip and fall because of that pothole the first couple times, but once you've run the route that avoids the pothole a few times, you won't even have to think about it. You'll just swerve around the pothole every time, without even consciously avoiding it.

Habits, once practiced for about 30 consecutive days, become engrained in your psyche. Your brain becomes trained to consider that habit normal, something that should be expected.

Applying These Concepts to Writing

Ask yourself this: *What are my current writing habits? Do you...*

- Think for a long time before you begin writing (each time)?
- Write for a few minutes, hit a detail that trips you up and then get derailed as you research online for that detail, losing focus and momentum?
- Write for a while, realize you don't have a plan or plot and then get stuck wondering if your book is going anywhere?
- Analyze your writing to the point that you aren't sure if you have any talent at all?
- These are all writing habits that will stop you from making progress.

You will need to establish writing habits that help you get words on the page. Then you'll need to establish habits that help you polish your work until it shines. You'll need habits that keep you organized and habits that keep you on track. All of these habits, when put together, will deliver results.

Don't Reinvent the Wheel

You might think that successful writers have all or most of the following:

- Unlimited time
- Unlimited inspiration
- A personal assistant who makes their coffee and picks up their kids from school

While some writers do have these things, the vast majority of successful writers started out just like you: working a full time job and writing in the time they designated for that purpose. *And how did they carve out that time?* They established a writing practice.

To demonstrate what I mean, here is an article that describes the daily writing habits of many popular (and successful) authors. http://bit.ly/1eow1Lm

- Stephen King writes 2000 words each day. He says "only under dire circumstances" does he allow himself to stop writing before he hits that 2000th word of the day.
- R.F. Delderfield wrote for a specific period of time each day—until four in the afternoon. Even if he finished a book mid-afternoon, he would stick a new piece of paper in his typewriter and start working on the next book, working until 4:00 in the afternoon.
- Jack London wrote between 1000 and 1500 words each day.

Every successful author develops a unique writing practice that suits his or her needs. As we'll discuss later, some writers perform best when they write in the early hours of the morning, while other authors write all night and sleep all day.

The key is this: They figure out how to produce material on a regular basis, and once they figure out their unique writing practice, they do it almost every single day.

The following chapters will cover 15 different writing habits you can use to crank out a consistent flow of content. As you read each chapter, make a note of how this specific writing habit will propel you towards your end goal—a finished book or two, and, more importantly, a workable writing practice.

Habit 1: Overcome Five Major Limiting Beliefs

Before you can do anything else, you need to establish a habit that deals with your biggest obstacle: *Your limiting beliefs.*

You may or may not know what these beliefs are, but you probably have some if you haven't already established a writing practice. Those beliefs are getting in your way of success, just like an 800-pound gorilla standing between you and your keyboard.

The following are limiting beliefs that will hinder your ability to turn writing into a permanent habit.

Read through this list, check the ones that you recognize and decide to daily replace the limiting belief with an affirmative statement. Post a list of these affirmative statements where you can quickly read through them at the beginning of your writing sessions.

1. I've always heard that fast writing is bad writing.

Replace this belief with the following affirmation: *Many successful writers are fast writers.*

While some writers swear by deliberate, careful writing, most successful writers plow through the first draft, leaving corrections to the second and third draft. It's important to put aside your internal editor and just get words down on the page when working on a first draft.

Check out how many words these famous authors cranked out:

- Erle Stanley Gardner (Perry Mason novels) – One million words a year
- John Grisham (legal thrillers) – One novel in 100 days, and another in six months
- Victor Hugo (Les Miserables, The Hunchback of Notre Dame) – 20 pages per day

Remember: You can always delete words you don't like, but you can't do anything with words that are still stuck in your head.

2. I will never make any money from writing.

Replace this belief with the following affirmation: *Plenty of authors make money from books they have self-published.*

There's a saying in the Internet world: "Content is king." Basically, all websites and businesses need one thing, and that is words! "Content" is anything from blog posts and web pages to ebooks and reports…and if it's good enough, people will be willing to pay for it.

Readers are willing to buy self-published books (print and digital), especially nonfiction written by subject experts. Fiction writers will want to consider approaching agents and publishers, but even fiction writers who are willing to self-promote can make decent money on self-published works.

Remember: You won't make money off a book that is still unwritten!

3. Nobody is interested in what I have to say.

Replace this belief with the following affirmation: *If I'm interested in it, there's an audience of people just like me who will appreciate it.*

While you should do research on the popularity of (or demand for) your subject matter, you really can't predict what people will be buying this year or the next. Instead, it's safer to write about topics you truly are interested in and know a lot about. Your authenticity will shine.

Remember: You can find a way to make even an obscure topic accessible and salable.

4. I can never figure out what to say.

Replace this belief with the following affirmation: *The words will come.*

This belief causes classic writer's block. If you learn how to research, plan and outline (all of which are addressed later in this book), you won't get stuck. You'll be able to sit down, glance at your outline and start writing.

Remember: You can overcome writer's block.

5. My writing (grammar, punctuation, structure) isn't good enough.

Replace this belief with the following affirmation: *I can always hire an editor or ask a friend to clean up my writing after I'm done.*

Many writers partner up with what they refer to as a "beta reader"—someone who critiques their work in exchange for a proofread of *their* work. This arrangement can provide insight, without costing any money.

If you don't want to spend time reading someone else's work, hire an editor or trade other goods or services for help from a friend or neighbor who has a good handle on English.

Remember: You need to write the book, but someone else can help you fine-tune it.

Your New Habit

Think through other limiting beliefs that may be getting in the way. Write up an affirmation that counters the limiting belief. Post this somewhere you can access it when starting your writing practice each day.

Okay, I'll admit this might seem a little hokey to some people. However, if you have an "inner voice" where you're filled with doubt, then it's important to immediately address this issue. While affirmations aren't for everybody, they can help you reprogram your mind to see things differently.

Habit 2: Establish a Daily Routine and Environment

"*I only write when I am inspired. Fortunately I am inspired at nine o'clock every morning.*" ~ William Faulkner

Many writers believe they should only write when they feel inspired. If you rely on this, you'll find that you are:

- Often inspired when you are too busy to write
- Almost never inspired when you have time to write

This happens to writers because they are actually afraid they might write something that isn't any good. That's why they feel inspired when they can't do anything about it, and don't feel inspired when they actually could write something. It's a way your subconscious protects you from writing crap and feeling bad about yourself.

Successful writers push past this fear and force themselves to get words on the page on a regular basis, inspired or uninspired. What they find is that after they write for a little while, the inspiration appears, even if they initially felt discouraged or anxious.

Why Do Routines Work?

Having a routine helps because once you force yourself to actually write something, your internal critic relaxes and lets you get down to business. (I'll explain more about how to turn off that internal critic later on.) After you write, you can go back and strip out the bad stuff. You can also polish the gems that remain. The end result is good writing.

The first step in silencing that internal critic is to set a routine so you know what to expect of yourself every single time you sit down to write.

If you don't have a routine established, you will waste a lot of time doing stuff like:

- Deciding where to sit
- Getting comfortable (and then deciding your initial spot wasn't comfortable, getting set up again, deciding that second location is not ideal, moving again, etc.)
- Figuring out what you want to write about
- Rethinking pages you already wrote
- Checking email, look at Facebook updates or surfing the web until you get in the mood to write
- Researching some insignificant fact that is only vaguely related to your book
- Basically doing anything other than writing

All of these actions can destroy your ability to complete 2,000 words on a daily basis. Instead, you need to establish a quality routine that includes the following:

- Five to seven days of writing. (Commit to a specific number of days per week.)
- A tracking plan (for word count, projects, locations and types of writing) to help you identify what factors help you write best.
- A regular time of day when you write. (You will need to play around with times of day to figure this out, but you should choose a time and stick with it once you know what time of day is best for you.)
- A place where you are free from distractions or interruptions.
- The habit of writing without thinking about it. Just sit down and go!

To help you develop an effective routine that works for you, I'll be discussing each of these factors of a good routine, broken down into individual habits.

Your New Habit

You'll combine several of the habits discussed in this chapter to form your writing routine. Then you'll need to make it a daily habit to actually perform this routine a specific number of days per week.

Habit 3: Schedule Time for Writing

Hopefully by now you've figured out that you need to make time to write instead of winging it. That means you'll choose a specific time to write each day and then commit to it. This daily time commitment is the first of the building blocks to creating a successful writing routine.

I like to write in the morning, a half hour after I wake up. I devote an hour to writing, five days a week, taking weekends off. This works for me because:

- I know I won't procrastinate and miss out on my writing hour because of unforeseen events or distractions.
- I'm most alert first thing in the morning. This is the time that works best for me.
- I spend that first half hour doing energizing activities that help me wake up and get motivated. [1]

---

[1] You can read about morning energizing activities in my book *Wake Up Successful*. The idea behind this ritual is to

What Time of Day Works Best for You?

You will want to play around with times of day until you figure out what works best for you. I've noticed that not all successful authors write at the same time of day. In fact, the following is true of these well-known writers:

- Stephen King writes in the morning and spends his afternoons relaxing, napping and taking care of personal business.
- John O'Hara wrote in the middle of the night and slept until the middle of the day.
- Rudyard Kipling wrote from late morning to late afternoon, about 10:00-4:00 each day.

You'll want to try writing at different times of day. Later on, we'll talk about the importance of tracking how much you got done and how you felt about your writing. This will help you determine what time works for you.

You may have to work around your work and personal schedule (kids, relationship), carving out time that works with the other demands in your life. This requirement may override your personal preference for writing. Take all of these factors into account as you choose a time of day.

---

build momentum and energy as I prepare for writing, so that by the time I sit down in front of my computer, I'm ready to work.

Schedule a Specific Time of Day

Once you've determined what time of day works best for you, you will need to set aside a specific time slot for writing each day. I suggest you reserve an hour each day, but you may need to set aside more or less time, depending on how much time it takes you to achieve your daily word count goal.

Once you've determined how much you can achieve in a set amount of time, you will want to add this to your daily schedule. For example, you could reserve 6:30–7:30 a.m. each morning for your writing habit. Pen it in, like a dentist appointment, and don't let anything come in the way.

Your New Habit

To make this choice into a habit, you will want to:

- Choose the same time every day.
- Repeat this habit every day (or every workday, if you are taking weekends off) for at least 30 days in a row.
- Schedule this time slot into your schedule book, blocking out all other commitments.
- Refuse to let anything (aside from true emergencies) push out your writing commitment.

Habit 4: Track Your Writing Routine

Good writers work in blocks of time, refusing to be distracted while they are "on the clock." They also carefully track their time, occasionally evaluating what environmental changes influence their ability to produce quality material at top speed.

To do this, you will want to master two writing habits: Writing in blocks of time and daily tracking your writing output.

Step #1: Track Blocks of Time

I first got the idea for writing in blocks of time when I noticed that my productivity dropped off at a particular point each day. I am able to write for a solid hour before needing to stop. However, when I wrote for more than one hour a day, I realized I worked more efficiently if I broke my writing down into smaller blocks of time.

This realization led me to exploring block writing techniques. That's when I stumbled across something that is called the *Pomodoro Technique*, a popular time blocking system that was created in the 1980s by Italian

Francesco Cirillo and is embraced by entrepreneurs and work efficiency experts alike.

The Pomodoro Technique is named after a popular timer that looks like a tomato (hence the name "pomodoro," which is Italian for tomato.) The timer was used like any old kitchen timer, but Cirillo experimented with time blocking until he discovered what is considered the most effective usage of time blocks (for efficiency in work production).

When using the technique, you will want to:
1. Choose a task.
2. Set a timer for 25 minutes.
3. Work for 25 minutes without any distractions, refusing to stop for anything.
4. Take a five-minute break.
5. Go back to work for another 25 minutes.
6. After every four time blocks (of 25 minutes of work and five minutes of a break), take a 15–30 minute break.

If you want to go high-tech with this, try using one of the following programs:
- Rapid Rabbit (iPhone and iPad apps) (http://rapidrabbit.de/pomodoro/)
- Flowkeeper (PC users) (http://sourceforge.net/projects/pomodorotimer/)
- Pomodoro (Mac users) (http://pomodoro.ugolandini.com/)
- Pomodoro (Android users) (http://android.hlidskialf.com/apps/pomodoro)

If you don't want to use the Pomodoro technique per se, try using a work-tracking program. These programs will ask you "Are you working?" when it appears you've gone off task, like checking Facebook.

You may want to experiment with time blocks other than the traditional 25 minutes on, 5 minutes off. Like I said, I work best for an hour first thing in the morning, but I need to break my writing efforts into smaller blocks of time after that first hour of the day passes. You may work best in half-hour blocks or with longer breaks.

Step #2: Track Your Writing

This leads right into my next point, which is the importance of tracking your writing habit. If you don't track how many words you produce and what environmental factors best affect your productivity, you will never discover your sweet spot. I've created a tracking form that has revolutionized my ability to track and evaluate my writing practice. It is a simple Excel spreadsheet that has eight columns:

1. Date
2. Time
3. Project name
4. Type of writing (outline, 1st draft, 2nd draft, etc.)
5. Blocks (or units of writing)
6. Word count
7. Average word count per block: Word count/blocks
8. Location

I record my information for the work period immediately after I finish writing. This way I can figure out if my productivity dropped at any particular point in time. After doing this for a while, I was able to determine that my two best productive times are first thing in the morning at the kitchen table and the occasional afternoons I spend at Starbuck's coffeehouse.

Creating *Your* Tracking Form

You'll want to create your own tracking form. You can use an Excel sheet, like I do, or you can print out a log or use an online tracking system. Whatever you choose, do it every time you write. I suggest you also write down why you didn't write if you skipped a day, or why you suspect you had poor productivity on days when you know you got derailed.

Be honest with yourself. Some common reasons for poor productivity are:

- Allowing family members to interrupt you
- Getting distracted by email or Facebook
- Researching a point and getting interested in something off-topic

If you call yourself on these distractions, you'll stop doing them. If you ignore your infractions and excuse them away, you'll repeat these bad habits.

The ultimate goal with all of this is to discover what makes you the most productive. Prolific writers have material to work with; skimpy writers have a much tougher time finishing a project. Discover the factors that make you the most productive and you'll find success.

Your New Habit

Work in blocks of time that you record on an Excel spreadsheet. Evaluate your productivity every two weeks. Look for patterns on those days when you can create a lot of words. Arrange your schedule so you do most of your writing in the time and location where you work best.

Habit 5: Find the Best Location

You might not think location matters much, but it truly has a direct impact on your ability to turn writing into a habit.

A good location is one where you can:

- Focus.
- Remain undisturbed.
- Feel inspired.
- Access locally (anything farther than 10 minutes from home or work isn't practical).

It's important to establish a primary place for your writing efforts. You will soon be conditioned to want to write whenever you enter that familiar space.

Home or Away?

Some writers work best at home, in familiar surroundings. Some find writing at home to be distracting since they have to ignore the laundry crying out to be folded and the kids squabbling on the other side of the house. Some writers love the white noise of restaurant patrons; others find the many surrounding conversations to be distracting.

You may be able to set up a special place in your home for writing. I have established two writing spots in my home—one for work-for-pay writing and one for creative writing. Having two spots helps me separate the one from the other. I experience a shift in mood and focus when I enter my sacred writing spots at home.

Option #1: Home

Explore the following options if you like to write at home:

- A formal office.
- A writing desk tucked away in a secluded corner in your home.
- The front porch (or back deck).
- Part of your bedroom.
- Convert a walk-in closet into a writing space.
- Use a foldable partition to separate out a writing space.

You may wish to decorate your writing space. This could include:

- List of writing affirmations
- Quotes from successful authors
- Pictures or quotes from experts in the topic you are covering
- A storyboard of your plot or outline of your book

- Photo ideas of characters in your book
- Pictures of writers who inspire you

You may also want to collect totems that inspire you. Set up your desk with all the writing supplies you could possibly need. I keep Post-It notes, an organizer, quality pens and a stapler next to my desk.

Why? Sometimes I print out information I find online. I need a place to keep that material where I can write on it, make notes about it and keep it organized so it is easily accessible but will not distract me. I don't keep any extraneous material on my desk—only writing materials—so that I'm never tempted to investigate a charge on my credit card or get lost in junk mail.

Option #2: Away

Explore the following options if you like to write away from home:

- Coffee shops, diners, bookstores, Panera Bread, Starbucks
- Office space in a co-working location
- Public places like a park

You will want to fill your laptop case with writing essentials for your writing excursions. When I write outside of my home, I bring a laptop, my outline, random notes and many pens. You may need to bring more writing aids with you if you tend to use them.

Some writers bring a totem with them wherever they go, just to get themselves in the mood to write. You may wish to keep a good luck charm or symbolic item on your writing desk that can be carried with you when you write outside the home.

How to Choose a Location

As you try out new locations, be sure to track them on your Excel file so you can measure productivity by location. You might "feel" more like an author when at a local coffee shop but actually get more done when alone in your office. The key is to find what works for *you*, not what other people suggest.

You will probably want to establish two places as your writing locations—one at home and one away from home. This will help you be flexible for days when you can't get out of the house or days when your home contains a gaggle of loud, rowdy family members.

One Pitfall to Avoid…

Warning: Don't allow yourself to become dependent on one location. If you do, you will run the risk of developing the mindset that you can only write in one special place.

This happened to me when I committed to writing in Starbucks every day. I stopped writing anywhere but in Starbucks, which impeded my ability to write every day. I had to retrain my brain to write in any location. A good writing habit is one where you can pull out a laptop and be able to work *anywhere*.

Your New Habit

Once you've chosen a location (or two,) make this your regular writing spot. Add it to your daily schedule.

For example, you might commit to writing at the local Panera Bread next to your work office from 7:00–8:00 a.m. each workday, right before you go to your job, which you start at 8:30 a.m., Monday through Friday. On weekends you might commit to writing from 9:00–10:00 a.m. in your home office.

Habit 6: Minimize Distractions and Interruptions

You might not think interruptions matter much, but they certainly do if you've got a limited amount of time to write each day. Writing requires concentration.

The Cost of Interruptions

Every time you get interrupted, you will lose a few minutes. This is because you lose your train of thought and then have to return to the project with a *"Where was I?"* type of thought. Studies say that it takes anywhere from 5 to 25 minutes to regain the level of focus you had before getting interrupted, depending on the level of interruption and depth of concentration required to complete a task.

When you've only got an hour or so a day to make progress, you need to keep that time sacred. That means you will need to take responsibility for preventing interruptions or distractions.

10 Ways to Minimize *Distractions*

Try the following strategies to minimize distractions:
1. Wear noise-canceling earphones.
2. Wear earplugs.
3. Listen to instrumental music.
4. Invest in a white noise machine and play it (most come with sounds like "ocean" or "rain" as well as generic white noise).
5. Work in a space where you can close the door and block out sounds from the rest of the house.
6. Sit in a remote part of a park, restaurant or coffee shop, away from loud talkers or groups.
7. Put on your blinders and refuse to look up from your computer screen when things happen around you.
8. Remind yourself that this is your sacred time; refuse to engage with the waitress or people in your household.
9. Clear your writing desk of all unnecessary items.
10. Silence your computer and phone so you won't hear the "ding" when you get a new email or text message.

9 Ways to Minimize *Interruptions*

Try the following strategies for avoiding interruptions:
1. Work in a quiet place or a place where it's easy for you to block out the actions of other people.
2. Talk to your roommates, significant other and/or children about your writing time. Make it clear that

you are not to be disturbed unless there is a true emergency.

3. Turn off your phone.

4. Work offline (so you won't be tempted to surf the web or get derailed by research).

5. Disconnect from email.

6. Post a sign on your office door that says, *"Please Do not Disturb Until ___ Time."*

7. Tell the waitress/waiter that you are working and won't need anything—assure them you will initiate if you need something.

8. Tell neighbors or friends who stop by that you are working to meet a deadline and can't talk right now.

9. Commit to working until you have worked for a set block of time.

Your New Habit

You will need to set yourself up for success. Describe your commitment to whoever might be tempted to interrupt you. Settle into your sacred place and use whatever aids you've chosen from the lists above (signs, earphones, etc.) to focus on writing and nothing but writing for your hour of power each day.

Habit 7: Create an Outlined Framework

Successful writers know that writer's block comes from an uncertainty about what to write. The best authors never experience this problem because they create specific processes that prevent this problem from happening. You will need to set up a framework that supports your writing, before you sit down to write.

For example:

- Nonfiction writers and bloggers use outlines.
- Fiction writers plot out their stories.
- Screenwriters use beats, scenes and acts.

I know there are a lot of writers who claim they work best without an outline. Perhaps this is true for them, but most successful writers need some sort of framework to lean upon.

A framework helps you remain on task because:

- You won't waste time wondering what the best next topic will be.

- You won't write a bunch of stuff that really doesn't matter, just to write something.
- You won't lose sight of the big picture.
- You will write material that makes sense, ties together well and follows a logical path.

This book, for example, started out as a list of bullet points. Those bullet points were organized into sensible chapters. I fleshed out those chapters, but the writing part of the project was easy because I had already decided what needed to be addressed and when I would address it. I moved chapters and paragraphs around when they were still in bullet point form, before I'd invested a lot of time and energy into writing the actual book.

Outlining and plotting is so important that we'll cover it in more detail in a later chapter.

Your New Habit

Force yourself to outline or plot out your book before you begin writing. Refuse to wing it any longer. Be prepared to spend *at least* a day or two to map out what you'll say before you sit down and start writing.

Habit 8: Focus on Small Writing Projects (at First)

'Write a short story every week. It's not possible to write 52 bad stories in a row." ~ Ray Bradbury

It's tempting to tackle a huge goal, like writing the ultimate authority book on a topic or "The Great American Novel."

The problem with this mindset is this: Most of us don't have the stamina to complete a huge project. Not on the first try. We need to experience success along the way or we lose steam.

Writing a novel, screenplay or large nonfiction book is very challenging. Massive books become unwieldy. They are tough to plot or plan out, and they usually require a great deal of time and mental energy to complete. It's hard to feel motivated when you've been working on the same project for the past year. Many people find that large projects suck the life out of them.

Where to Start?

Instead of trying to write the modern-day *War and Peace*, create small pieces of work, and then use these to scale into larger projects.

EXAMPLE:

- If you want to write a screenplay, don't try to create the next *Titanic*. Instead, make that small budget Indie film that people love.
- Write short stories or a novella before you tackle a full-scale novel. There's no shame in publishing a handful of short stories or self-publishing a novella. In fact, this will give you a chance to find out which medium suits you best as you hone your writing skills.
- Instead of trying to fill an entire website's worth of material, try blogging two to three times a week or tackling a web page per day.
- Tackle a short eBook on a topic you know well before taking on a longer or more advanced eBook that will require a great deal of research and quoting of sources.

Keep Your Eye on the End Goal

Remember, you're trying to build a sustainable writing habit. If you take on too daunting of a project, you'll:

- Burn out before you finish
- Get lost in the details
- Lose interest in the topic

- Possibly write something that is so convoluted or complex that it isn't salable
- Potentially give up on writing altogether

Instead, your goal is to build momentum by creating a writing habit where you <u>always reach the finish line</u>. As you set and meet small goals, you'll build towards reaching larger goals. You may even be able to string the smaller projects together to create a massive book—all of which make sense and work together.

Your New Habit

Break large goals into small, achievable projects with reasonable deadlines. Celebrate when you finish each small project. Get feedback from others and use it to steer the course of what you'll create next.

Habit 9: Turn Writing into a Profit Center

The ultimate litmus test of a written piece of work is to ask people to pay for it. There's nothing like the rush of getting that first paycheck or making that first sale.

Monetary compensation will reinforce your writing habit and propel you into subsequent projects, providing internal motivation to keep writing. If you can establish a positive relationship that links your daily writing habit to making money (or meeting another measurable goal, like how many followers you have), you will be more likely to finish your writing project and continue writing.

I've made money with my words in a variety of ways, so I can attest that it's a viable business model. Here are a few ideas to get your creative juices flowing:

Idea #1: Self-Publish

One of the best ways I've found to generate income from writing is to self-publish. Now don't get me wrong; I'm **not** saying it's easy to make money from self-published works.

There's a lot to it, from formatting and promoting your work to building a following and a reputation—but it's a lot easier today than it was a decade ago. The tools you need are readily available, and the skills needed are easy to learn. You just need to get ahold of a good guide and do the work required to get your book published and noticed.

Kindle publishing is my favorite vehicle for self-publishing. As I mentioned before, I've published 35 books, and I will continue to build upon this library. Right now, Amazon is the top place to quickly publish, get feedback from customers and refine your writing process.

If you'd like to know more about how I operate my Kindle publishing business, I recommend you check out my "Steve Scott" author page (http://www.ebooksbysteve.com/) , which has a variety of titles on this subject.

If you're looking to write a novel or set of short stories, I'd encourage you to read the book, _Write. Publish. Repeat.,_ which is put together by the guys at _The Self-Publishing Podcast_. (One bit of warning—they love to curse on this show, so don't listen to it at work or if you have kids around.)

The fiction market is a little tougher to break into than the nonfiction market, but it can be more financially rewarding if you're willing to work hard and learn from each book you publish.

Idea #2: Blogging, Affiliate Marketing, Information Products

I'll tread lightly over this subject, because many people feel that any "make money online" opportunity is a scam. Truth is, there are a number of ethical ways to generate an Internet income. Again, it requires hard work and a lot of dedication.

There are a lot of sites where you can learn the principles of running an Internet business. My suggestion is to start with the sites that teach you how to do it in a straightforward, honest manner:

- Internet Business Mastery (http://internetbusinessmastery.com/)
- Niche Pursuits (http://nichepursuits.com/)
- Smart Passive Income (http://www.smartpassiveincome.com/)
- Empire Flippers (http://empireflippers.com/)
- Authority Case Study (http://authoritycasestudy.com/)

You can build a viable business online, but there are a lot of sharks in the waters. My suggestion is to check out the free content on these sites and educate yourself before spending a dollar. That way you'll know if a specific program or tool is worth the monetary investment.

Idea #3: Freelance Writing

Freelance writing is a business model many use to make money with their words. Instead of developing a website from scratch, you build a database of clients who hire you to create blog posts, articles and eBooks. Now, I've never been a freelance writer. However, my friend Tom Ewer (of *Leaving Work Behind*) supports himself through his freelance writing. <u>You can read about his experiences on his blog.</u>

Idea #4: Traditional Publishing

If you have written a piece of fiction and aren't sure you want to tackle the self-promotion required to make money off your work, submit your work to a literary journal (for short stories or poems), contest, agent or publisher.

You will need to learn the proper format for submitting. One resource is the free writing forum <u>Absolute Write</u>. And you could also check out the submission website <u>Query Tracker</u> to learn the proper way to submit your work.

Your New Habit

Develop a workmanlike attitude towards your writing. Don't wait around for inspiration. Treat it like a job where you put effort in, get results and hopefully make a little bit of money.

Trust me—there's nothing more motivating than seeing income come in from your written words.

Habit 10: Focus on One Project at a Time

If you're like me, you've got a lot of projects spinning in your mind. You'd love to build a dozen websites or write several books. You get excited about multiple topics and want to write about all of them—*right now*.

The problem is this: Most overly ambitious writers end up with a pile of half-written projects instead of a handful of completed works. If you want to succeed, you will need to work on one project at a time, finishing one project before you start another.

Creating a Production Model

Most successful writers come up with a **production model** that allows them to crank out project after project. They stick with this model even if they suddenly get inspired to start a new project. Why? Because they understand the value of a completed project.

Compare the following…

Option A: 15 Uncompleted/Half-Finished Projects

- Can't sell to readers or clients.
- Can't submit to agents or publishers.

- Can't relax and stop thinking about these projects.

Option B: Three Completed Projects

- Probably making money off them, even if it's just a small amount from each one.
- Have something professional to submit to agents or publishers, refer to on Amazon or post on your portfolio.
- Can focus on one project, giving it all of your attention.

Which do you think is the more sustainable model?

Obviously, you will be more motivated to actually write every day if you have completed works to reference. Every completed project will build your confidence. Every half-finished project will erode your motivation.

The Importance of "Batching" Multiple Projects

In an ideal situation, you'd work on one project, finish it completely and then move on to another project. However, I realize that some projects naturally lead to multiple other projects.

EXAMPLE:

- **If you write an eBook**, you'll probably want to create a website to support sales of that eBook. The website will require you to write static web pages. You'll also probably want to write blog posts to drive traffic to the website. If you're smart, you'll probably also find a way to gather email addresses from people who visit your site and then reach out to those people through email campaigns.

- **If you write a novel**, you'll probably need to maintain an author website and blog. You will also need to interact via social media, posting on a Facebook page and tweeting.

You probably won't get to just forget about your first completed project and move onto eBook or novel number two.

When you need to complete multiple projects, batch them into achievable segments. Tackle each segment one at a time so you can finish one segment before you move on to another.

EXAMPLE:

If you need to write another eBook, blog posts for your website and autoresponders (for email campaigns), you might want to set up a schedule that looks like this:

- Write and post blog posts (for the month—just schedule them to post at later dates) during week one of the month.
- Write and schedule autoresponder messages during week two of the month.
- Write the eBook during weeks three and four.

Bundling Small Projects

This really gets tricky when you need to move from one distinctly unique project to another.

Let's say you've written a novel and you need to write all the supporting material (web pages, blog posts, social media material) to support that novel, and now you're working on a series of short stories. You might feel like there is just too much conflicting material to be able to finish any one project.

This is where bundling of material by topic can be helpful. You will want to work on all your "novel stuff" for half the month, and then put it all aside while you focus on your "new short story series stuff" for the last two weeks of the month. This way you are bundling material such that you get to think about the mini-projects as one project. This will keep you from feeling scattered.

The same bundling technique works well for entrepreneurs who have several websites going. Perhaps you own several unrelated affiliate websites. You might have one website that caters to parrot owners, another site that speaks to working mothers and yet another that caters to homeowners who like do-it-yourself projects. You will want to divide your attention such that you knock out all the parrot stuff in one week, the working moms stuff another week and the DIY stuff in a third week.

This sort of bundling will allow you to think about one topic at a time.

Your New Habit

Instead of jumping from project to project as you feel inspired, force yourself to complete one project (or, at the very least, a subset of that project) before moving on to another. Create distinct boundaries so you can focus completely on the project at hand before you start another project.

Habit 11: Create an Energized Writing State

One of the things you need to fuel a sustainable writing habit is energy. Some people imagine energy just comes and goes, that inspiration is an ethereal state. They even refer to this energy as a muse.

The good news is this: You don't have to wait for the muse to appear. You can create energy for writing by deliberately engaging in simple activities that build writing energy. You will also want to make lifestyle changes that will increase your baseline energy. By doing this, you will find that motivation and enthusiasm are within reach every day.

10 Ways to Create Energy for Writing

Try the following strategies:

1. Immerse yourself in your subject. Listen to podcasts about the subject, read competing works and talk to people about it. The information you glean will provide inspiration.

2.   Find a writing partner who challenges and inspires you.

3.   Reread parts of your writing that you are particularly proud of.

4.   Check your sales records or reread your contract with your agent or publisher.

5.   Read related publications, like *Publisher's Marketplace*.

6.   Read in your genre. For example, if you want to write short stories, subscribe to the *New Yorker* and read the fiction pieces.

7.   Befriend an established writer.

8.   Post inspirational quotes by your writing space.

9.   Expose yourself to other artists or experts in your field. Fiction writers may find inspiration from musicians; nonfiction writers may get fired up after attending a conference or *MeetUp*.

10. Think about your project as you fall asleep at night. You'll work on your project as you sleep, waking up refreshed and ready to write!

Lifestyle Changes that Will Increase Your Baseline Energy

You will want to make the following changes to your lifestyle:

•   Eat healthfully. Your diet affects your energy level. If you don't know how to change your eating habits, get help from a dietitian.

•   Get a full night's rest every night. It's hard to write well when you're sleep deprived.

- Exercise regularly. Exercise increases blood flow to the brain, enhancing your ability to focus and think clearly. Choose a form of exercise that allows you to think about your projects.
- Running, walking, biking and swimming are all perfect for writers—you can plot out a chapter or work on an outline while performing these exercises because they don't require a lot of focus or interaction with other people.
- Create a morning wake-up routine that fuels your writing habit.
- Take naps when you can. I love 'em!

Never underestimate the power of energy in relation to your writing habit. Forget about the notion of writing like Hemingway with a bottle of whiskey in your hand. The most prolific writers understand the importance of harnessing a positive, energized state.

Your New Habit

Explore ways to improve your energy levels. Once you've determined what activities energize you the most, incorporate them into a regular routine. Don't be afraid to play around with different things to see what works for you. This will help you determine the activities that leave you fresh and ready to write.

Habit 12: Touch Type to Increase Writing Speed

How many fingers do you use to type? Two fingers? Four? Six? How many errors do you make in a typical sentence? If you're still hunting and pecking, it's time to learn how to touch type.

There are several reasons why the hunt-and-peck method isn't going to cut it anymore:

- Touch typists can produce, on average, 40 words per minute.
- Typical hunt-and-peck typists produce 25 words per minute.
- Good touch typists produce over 60 words per minute.

Obviously, when you are short on time, *faster is better.*

Touch typists also make fewer errors. This is important because:

- Correcting errors is frustrating.
- Correcting errors ruins your train of thought and derails productivity.

- Correcting errors takes time.

Typing Class? Ugh!

If your initial reaction was to groan and skip over this chapter, you probably need to take this challenge. Take the time today to:

- Time yourself while typing.
- Count how many errors you made in your one-minute typing test.
- Consider how much more you would produce each year if you took this one challenge.

You don't have to enroll in a community college class to learn how to touch type. There are several software packages available that will teach you how to touch type. One of my favorites is the *Mavis Beacon* program (http://www.developgoodhabits.com/mavis) that I used to learn as a teenager.

Tried Before and Failed?

Have you attempted to teach yourself to touch type in the past but failed? Take my 30-Day Habit Challenge and dedicate the next month to developing this habit:

Your New Habit

Refuse to hunt and peck any longer. Force yourself to touch type—even when doing personal correspondence—until touch typing is all you do. Sure, you might lose some writing time to learn this habit, but this investment is worth it because you'll make up for it as you become a proficient typist.

Habit 13: Develop Enthusiasm for Your Projects

Enthusiasm is extremely important for your writing habit. If you aren't truly interested in the topic, you won't produce high word counts. Your mind should be spilling over with ideas related to your project. If you find yourself bored or procrastinating, you will want to explore new ways to increase your enthusiasm.

Is this the Right Project?

If writing feels like a chore, ask yourself these three questions:

- Q1: Am I working on the right writing project?
- Q2: Is there another topic about which I am more passionate?
- Q3: Could this project be spun off into something else--something that captivates me more?

You may discover that you will have more natural enthusiasm if you alter or change your project focus. You may discover that, while you are excited about instructing people how to do a specific activity, you get bored when researching the history of the topic or theoretical aspects of the subject. Conversely, you may realize that you are into the big idea or grand concepts, but are not good at describing practical "how-to" guides.

EXAMPLE:

Let's say you start a website about gardening tips and find yourself stuck whenever you try to write about fencing or pest control. On the other hand, you're interested in talking about what type of plants to grow in your home climate. Perhaps you can steer the direction of your site towards that ultra-specific subject. You also may realize that you have taken on too big of a project. If you set out to write a novel but are losing steam, consider breaking it down into several short stories, all of which are related. Look for ways to shorten, alter or revamp your project to make it something you are truly excited to work on.

7 Ways to Cultivate Enthusiasm

In many cases, you simply need to feed your enthusiasm. Think of your passion as a small flame flickering inside your psyche. Every piece of information is like a piece of kindling. Feed it and the fire will grow.

You will want to do some of the following activities to feed your enthusiasm:

- Meet with experts in your field.
- Watch webinars or videos about your topic.

- Watch movies about your topic.
- Read books that are related to your subject.
- Subscribe to blogs of others who know a lot.
- Look for ways to try out ideas or theories covered in your book.
- Make your topic as practical and applicable to your life as possible.

Specifically, you can further break this down into actions based on what *type* of writing you'd like to do.

Fiction writers will want to:
- Meet other fiction writers who have succeeded (look into writing groups, workshops, conferences, writing events.)
- Interview people who are like characters in your book (police, DNA analysts, FBI agents, etc.)
- Read fiction that inspires you.
- Watch movies that have the same feel as your book.

Nonfiction writers will want to:
- Meet up with experts who know your topic.
- Try experiments (for example, Tim Ferriss, the author of *Four Hour Body* and *The Four Hour Workweek*, tried different products and techniques, keeping records of results so he could write with authority).
- Visit worksites, research labs and historical sites.
- Experience as much as you can firsthand.

The more you *immerse* yourself in the subject matter, the more you'll develop the enthusiasm to improve the quality of your writing.

Your New Habit

Immerse yourself in your topic. Use all your senses as you explore your subject matter and feed the fire of your enthusiasm. Experiment with your writing projects to make sure you're doing what you love.

Habit 14: Keep an Idea Book

Ever get ideas when you're unable to write? What happens when you don't jot them down? Usually they'll vanish from your mind.

The key to continuous idea generation is to use *external* stimulations. You may get inspired by a painting you see or an interaction between two people at the grocery store. You might realize you've got your marketing principles all wrong once you see a good advertisement on TV, or while discussing a topic with a friend.

Some of us need to spend time doing what's commonly called a "flow activity" in order for ideas to gel. Flow activities are activities that allow your subconscious to work on a thought.

They are usually activities that are repetitive and do not require much concentration, like mowing the lawn, going on a road trip or painting a room. This is why you get good ideas while out on a walk or bike ride. Others of us get ideas while in the shower, at work or sleeping. You may wake up with an idea in the middle of the night, but realize you don't have the energy to actually write a chapter or scene.

This is why you want to **start an idea book**, jotting down every possible thought.

Why Idea Books Work

You might think it's kind of corny to keep an idea book, but you'll be amazed at how useful this can be. As you jot down one idea, you'll often find out that there is a second, or even third and fourth idea attached to that first idea. Sometimes the jotting of a single note will turn into a mini-brainstorming session, resulting in an entire scene or chapter.

The capturing of a resource or idea is also very helpful. What might have dissipated into an unusable wisp of an idea can be turned into a solid, practical point or chapter.

How to Make the Idea Book a Regular Habit

You won't want to haul around a big old clunky notebook, but you will be able to make note-taking a habit if you invest in a pocket-sized notebook or a mobile phone app. An idea book works if you:

- Carry it everywhere you go.
- Add to it constantly.
- Refer to it at least once a month.
- Deliberately engage in activities that stir up ideas for you.

I find that exercise is one of my best idea-stirring activities. I exercise daily—because it's good for me physically, of course, but also because it's good for my projects. I get ideas almost every time I exercise. I've made it a habit to jot down ideas after every run or walk.

Get the Right Tools

In addition to a pocket-sized notebook, you'll want online tools.

When doing research online, keep notes using Evernote (http://www.evernote.com/), which is an online resource that allows you to capture URLs, snippets from web pages and your personal notes online—forever. You can use Evernote on your mobile device as well, creating an online compilation of all your notes for your writing project.

Your New Habit

Carry your idea book with you everywhere you go. Get in the habit of jotting down ideas whenever they come to you. Don't second-guess these thoughts. Even if something sounds silly, jot it down because it might lead to something incredible.

Habit 15: Create a Writing Process

This habit is the most important of them all. I've even devoted the remainder of this book to teaching you how to develop a writing process that is repeatable and reliable.

Once you've created a process that can be repeated each time you sit in front of the computer, you'll find yourself writing faster and more easily. The writing process will make it easy to complete this habit without delay each and every day.

In the most basic of terms, your writing process will look like this:

- Outline
- Research
- Write 1st draft
- Write 2nd draft
- Write 3rd draft
- Edit
- Polish

Following this process will help you <u>avoid writer's block</u>. Why? Writer's block occurs when you are trying to access both sides of your brain at the same time. This is because you have:

1. **The creative side of your brain.** This is the side that helps you think of plots, ideas and important points. You will need to access the creative side of your brain when you are writing your outline and your rough drafts.

2. **The editing side of your brain.** This side of your brain is critical and often gets in the way of the production of creative work. However, it is essential for cleaning up your work after you've written it.

Why Use a Process?

Very few writers can write and proof their work at the same time. You will need to learn a process that allows you to turn off your editor brain while your creative brain gets all the good stuff down on paper. Then you'll want to turn off your creative brain and let your editor brain polish your work until it shines.

Having a process may seem like extra work, but it's one of the key elements to a consistent writing habit. This process will teach you how to shut off your critical brain when outlining and writing first drafts. It will also teach you how to stop creating when you need to edit and polish your work into something salable.

How Does the Process Work?

Each step in this process has a purpose:

1.   Outline – This is when you let your creative brain dump out all your thoughts on a subject. You will then organize those thoughts into an outline that makes sense of the jumbled ideas.

2.   Research – Look for links, quotes, definitions and concepts that support your outline. Some people will choose to research before outlining, using the information collected in the research stage in the brainstorming part of outlining.

3.   Write 1st draft – Use a stream of consciousness type of writing to just get the words down on the page. Do not worry about grammar, flow, structure or spelling.

4.   Write the 2nd draft – You will now read through what you've written, reading for content (not grammar.) You will use this draft to reorganize, add supporting material and make sure each chapter makes sense.

5.   Write the 3rd draft – You will now read through your material, cutting out extraneous material and adding more supportive points or details. You will also edit for grammar, punctuation and spelling in this draft. Check facts and sources.

6.   Editing – Hire a professional editor to go over the material. It's very difficult to catch your own mistakes.

7.   Final Proof – Look over the edits made by the professional editor and make final changes. This is the last polish.

Your New Habit

Commit to the process, working through each step to completion before allowing yourself to advance to the next step. Stick to the process and you will never struggle with writer's block again.

To learn how to fully integrate this final habit, let's go over each component of the process.

Process Component 1: Outlining

Does outlining make you nervous? Have you convinced yourself you are a "pantser"—in other words, someone who doesn't need to use an outline?

I also used to dislike the idea of writing an outline. However, after much experimenting, I've come to realize that outlining is:

- Not as hard as it sounds
- *The* way to quickly write a book

Why is an outline the best way to prevent writer's block? If you have a solid outline, you'll never struggle with what to write again. I'm going to teach you how to quickly write a foolproof outline in four steps:

Step #1: Come up With a Hook

You need to figure out why people will want to read your content. Then, once you know who your audience is and what they will want, you can write it all down, just scribbled down on an index card or two. Tape those index cards by your bathroom mirror or computer monitor and think about your hook for the next week, letting ideas multiply as you go about your daily business.

You will want to read your hook before you go to bed at night, exercise or perform any other mundane task (such as mowing the lawn, painting a room or staining your back deck). Your subconscious mind will go to work, stirring up ideas. It will tap into the recesses of your mind. You will suddenly notice things that inspire you everywhere you go—kind of like how it works when you learn a new vocabulary word and suddenly you hear other people using it or see things that exemplify that word.

Step #2: Brainstorm for a Week

Take out a notebook or open a Word document. Now engage in a total brain dump—meaning you write down every single idea you have for your book.

To perform an effective brainstorm session, you will want to write down everything you can think of as fast as you can. Make sure you:

- Don't stop to correct spelling or grammar.
- Don't elaborate—just jot down bullet points.
- Don't censor ideas because they seem stupid or irrelevant.
- Get down even incomplete seeds of ideas.
- Make notes like "research this idea" for untested concepts.
- Don't worry about how you'll work a particular idea into the book, or if it even fits.

You just want to get as many ideas down as possible.

If possible, dedicate a week to this step. This will help you think of additional ideas that you might not have considered in the original brainstorming session.

Some people like to do a mind map, but I find the structure causes me to hesitate and lose valuable ideas. You might want to try both and see what works best for you. Wikipedia has a great overview of the mind mapping process (http://en.wikipedia.org/wiki/Mind_map).

When you run out of ideas, put down your pen (or save your Word document) and walk away. If you come up with more ideas, jot them down in your idea book and add them to the list when you sit down to perform Step #3.

Step #3: Write Your Outline

I like to use index cards to write out my outlines, but you might prefer to go straight to outlining in a Word document. Let me explain *how* I use an index card system to create books that practically write themselves:

Break Your Ideas Down Into Chapters

Get a pack of index cards (lined on one side, blank on the other side). Using your brainstorming points, divide your ideas into nine to twelve chapters. In other words, choose nine to twelve main ideas from your list of bullet points.

Write these chapter ideas on index cards (on the blank side). You can write them as chapter titles or as questions. For example, this chapter started as an index card titled *"How do I use outlining to avoid writer's block?"*

Use Your Supporting Ideas for Sub-Chapters

Now go through your leftover ideas and see if they fit neatly into your nine to twelve chapters. Write each of these ideas on an individual index card and file it under the chapter heading index card. When possible, frame the idea as a question. In some cases you will want to write out individual steps as sub-chapters.

As you go through this process, you may discover you need to add one more chapter head or combine two chapters into one. You may also end up crossing out ideas you realize won't really work for this book (but may be perfect for another book in the future.)

Flesh out Each Sub-Chapter

You'll end up with somewhere between 27 and 60 index cards, each of which represents a chapter or sub-chapter of your book.

Take each index card that represents a sub-chapter and flip it over to the lined side. Write the more important points you will cover in that sub-chapter. This should look like three to five sentences for each sub-chapter.

When you've finished doing this for every sub-chapter, you will have an entire ebook outlined.

Step #4: Create Your Outline

Now you can transfer the information from your index cards into a Word document. As you do so, you may realize that you need to move chapters or sub-chapters around. You may also find inspiration to add in more sub-points, or even to divide one chapter into two.

As you do this, you will want to:

- Get rid of redundant ideas or combine good ideas to make one strong point instead of three repetitive and weak points.
- Ditch points that don't really add value.
- Highlight areas where you need to do research or come up with more supporting evidence.
- Make notes to yourself about adding illustrations, coming up with metaphors or otherwise fleshing out an idea.

Some writers prefer to keep the index cards instead of writing it out as a Word document. If you like this process, then figure out how to order your index cards and keep them in an ordered pile or a few ordered stacks.

You may even want to use a wall as a storyboard, taping your index cards on the wall (with the supporting points below the chapter head index cards.) Then you can move cards around and replace them as you see fit.

Plotting for Fiction Writing...

If you are writing a short story, novella, novel or screenplay, you will want to follow this same process but organize according to plot line or beats. You will also want to create a detailed character list with profiles of every character, including but not limited to:

- Physical descriptions (many writers include illustrations or pictures).
- Important biographical information such as age, birthplace, occupation and personality traits.
- Description of motive.
- Description of role in storyline.
- Notes on the important events that need to take place.

You will also want to include a write-up of important big picture information, such as notes on:

- Time period
- Location
- Culture
- Environmental factors

These are pages you will refer to often. Most fiction writers like to post them on the wall or create a folder that they can bring with them when writing away from home. Also, many fiction writers swear by the software program Scrivener (http://www.literatureandlatte.com/scrivener.php) to keep track of all the important notes related to a particular story.

Whether you're a nonfiction or fiction author, you'll find it's easy to overcome writer's block by using an outline with every piece of content you create.

Process Component 2: Research

As you jot on index cards or create your Word document, you'll probably discover many holes in your manuscript. You might need to reference experts or sources; you may also need to look up statistics or study results.

Go back through your index cards or outline and fill in the missing information. Research answers online; call sources. Get your facts verified (and make note of where you found the information in case you need to cite sources later).

Beware of getting off track while researching. This is one part of the process that can be dangerous. Many a writer has gotten off track while researching. It's a way many of us procrastinate. Remember: You have committed to killing the procrastination tendency in your life. You can do that by committing to the following:

- Set a timer when researching. Allow yourself 10 minutes per fact/topic that you need to research. When the timer goes off, check to make sure you didn't get off topic or distracted by something unimportant.

- Turn researching into a game. You should have a specific list of things you need to research. Jot down the time you start researching a topic and then find the information you need. Document the answer, jot down the time again and start on the second issue requiring research. Race against yourself; the goal is to get as much research done as possible in a short period of time.

When you've got all the holes in your outline filled, you are ready to write your rough draft.

Process Component 3: Write the First Draft

This is the point where a lot of writers get stuck. For some reason, they build up the first draft in their minds to be this big deal. They want to write the perfect manuscript right off the bat. They fear bad writing.

Your challenge is to ignore the critical editor brain that tempts you to stop and edit as you write. Instead, you need to tell yourself this important truth:

It does not matter how good or bad your first draft is.

What matters is that you get that first draft *completed.*

How to Write a First Draft

Believe or not, it's simple to write a first draft (the hard part comes later). You need to commit to a specific amount of time each day, and when you sit down to write, you simply elaborate on your outline. The key to writing (and not getting stuck with writer's block) is to do the following:

- Follow the outline.

- Refuse to question or alter the outline.
- Refuse to edit for spelling, grammar or even wording.
- Write notes to yourself about what you need to do to make this chapter work. (Use "comments" if you don't like to write inside the text to yourself.)
- Write using sloppy language (if that's what works for you.)
- Write more than what you think is necessary (and make a note to yourself saying "Condense later"), or write in bullet points if you can't bring yourself to flesh something out.
- Allow yourself to skip anything that doesn't come to you quickly.

This last point is important. Those parts of the manuscript that trip you up are like speed bumps, only more dangerous. They are the roots of writer's block.

How to Handle Speed Bumps

As you write, you will hit spots where you don't know what you should say. Instead of agonizing over the writing at these points, do the following:

- Write, "Note to self: Write this later!"
- Make note of what other research you might need to do, writing, "Research this" or asking a specific question to be researched.
- Write, "Clean this up later."
- Write, "Maybe cut this?"

Whatever you decide, don't stop writing. Never sit there, wondering what to do next. Just make a note to yourself, return to your outline and start writing again.

How to Overcome the Recurring Speed Bumps

If you discover you are having a hard time with a lot of points, you may need to make a note, saying something like:

- *"Maybe combine this chapter with this other chapter?"* if you are having trouble writing the material because you realize it is redundant.
- *"Not working. Possibly cut this chapter?"*
- *"Off topic?"*
- *"Too boring? Maybe needs to be condensed?"*

Then move along in the outline until you find something you can write about.

If you still can't get into writing, you may need to revise your outline. Just take the time to revise, and then get started again. Whatever you do, don't give up on the project.

How to Silence the "Editor Brain"

As you write, you will be tempted to revise, polish, criticize or worry that you are writing garbage. This is normal. Every single writer experiences this from time to time.

When this happens, you need to silence that inner critic. You can overcome the critic by reminding yourself:

- *"This is just a rough draft. It's not supposed to be good."*
- *"This is a work in progress. I'm supposed to have holes and incomplete thoughts."*
- *"I am the only person who will see this draft. I don't need to worry about what anyone else will think."*

Stephen King suggests writing rough drafts with the door to your office closed. Why? He says this helps him psychologically—he feels like he can make his mistakes in private, where he is not thinking about someone else looking over his shoulder.

Write What You'd Want to Read

As you're writing, imagine yourself as the reader. *What would you want to know about this subject? How would you want to learn about it? What story do you want to tell? How do you want the reader to experience the story?*

Relax and enjoy yourself as you share your knowledge with your imaginary audience.

As you read each cue card (index card) for a nonfiction book, ask yourself:

- How can I show this instead of telling? (Look for real-life examples to write about.)
- Is there a step-by-step process I should share here? (If so, write out instructions, broken down into easy-to-follow steps.)
- Can I think of an imaginary scenario that would make my point?

- Do I have personal experience with this topic? (If so, share it.)
- How can I make this point clear and simple? (Look for ways to simplify information.)

As you read each cue card for your fiction piece, ask yourself:

- How does this move the plot along?
- How does this scene tie into the one before it and lead into the one following it?
- Which character is being developed in this scene?
- How am I entertaining the reader? Will the reader be thrilled? Intrigued? Moved to tears? (Aim to create an emotional response with each segment of the story.)
- Have I followed the proper screenplay structure? Where is the laugh? The romance? The chase scene? Follow the established screenplay structure to stay on track.

Remember: Don't worry about craftsmanship while you write your rough draft. Focus instead on getting the story down or sharing your knowledge, reminding yourself that you will polish it up later. Make sure you cover every point on your outline and convey the most significant information.

The most important thing is to get the draft written. This is what matters when you're writing a first draft.

Process Component 4: Write the Second Draft

Your second draft is the place where you shift gears from creative brain to editor brain. It's a good idea to take a break for a day or two before starting the next version. Spend time brainstorming the next project or reading something in your genre before you dive back into writing.

Once you're ready to dive into your second draft, remind yourself that:

- The writing will feel clunky or disjointed.
- You will have a lot of work to do.
- It's *okay* that you have a lot of work to do.

How to Perform a Heavy Edit

During your second draft, you will probably change a lot of things. Writers tend to vary on how they like to perform a second draft, dividing into two camps.

#1. Red Pen Camp

These are the writers who like to print out a hard copy of the manuscript and then read through it in one swoop, pretending they are the audience, highlighting poor writing and making notes with a red pen.

#2. Dive-Right-Into-Editing Camp

These are the writers who like to perform a heavy edit without reading through the whole thing first. They're the folks who want to get their hands dirty right away, who can't stand to see mistakes.

I happen to be in the dive-right-into-editing camp, but there's really no right or wrong way to do this. Read through it and make notes on a hard copy if that works for you, or dive right into editing if that works for you.

In either case, you'll start working on your second draft, during which you will:

- Reword awkward sentences.
- Simplify long paragraphs.
- Cut extra words.
- Check facts.
- Add hyperlinks.
- Flesh out empty spots.
- Insert examples.
- Move stuff around.
- Cut anything that doesn't fit.
- Check grammar rules.

- Check your spelling.

Your second draft may take longer to write than your first draft. Why? Because this is the draft in which you get all the facts right. It's the draft that makes you call up that expert you interviewed and make sure you quoted him right. It's the draft that requires research and agonizing over the wording.

The great thing is this: You already have the content written, so it's not nearly as hard as writing that first draft. So, while the second draft is more painstaking, it doesn't require creative thinking like the first draft.

Process Component 5: Write the Third Draft

Once you've finished the second draft, you'll have a manuscript that's close to perfect. Still, you'll have work to do, especially if you weren't so diligent with the second draft. Now it's time to go through your book and make sure it's really ready to go.

Step 1: Add All Extra Material

This is the point when you will want to add:

- A title page, credits, bibliography, resources
- Pages and links that will help you get more traffic to your site or make more sales
- Window dressing, like quotes, images and illustrations

I personally believe in adding as little as possible. Make sure every extra link or page you add will enhance the value and salability of the book. Ask yourself: *How will this make the book better?* If you can't find a good answer to that question, don't add the page or link in question.

Step 2: Read it out Loud

You will be surprised how many missed words will show up when you read a book out loud. You'll be able to correct awkward writing and revise dialogue such that it sounds natural as you read. You will also probably identify extra material that doesn't add value to the book. Cut extra words, and even extra paragraphs if necessary.

Step 3: Find Someone to Proofread Your Book

You might think this is going overboard, but there's good reason for this step.

An outside reader will give you perspective you would otherwise miss. You will want to choose someone who is:

- Well versed in English
- Honest and objective
- Positive about your endeavor (and not just out to criticize for the sake of criticizing)
- Representative of your goal audience
- Willing to prioritize your book (so you're not waiting for months for feedback)

Fiction writers need to be particularly picky about who they choose as a reader. If you have written a novel, you will need to find a novelist who writes in your genre to review your book. If you have written a screenplay, make sure you find a screenplay writer. Your buddy who writes ebooks for a living won't know what to expect from a screenplay, and your best friend who reads fantasy novels won't know how to critique literary fiction.

How to Deal with Negative Feedback

It's important to take criticism seriously. Remember:

- You chose this person to review your book for a reason.
- You need honest feedback.
- You want the book to be the best it can be.

Read through the critique with an open mind. If your reader wasn't able to follow your logic, you need to clarify points. If your reader was bored, you need to condense extraneous material. If your reader didn't find your book believable, you need to bolster your claims with facts and studies. If your reader says your writing is clunky, you may need to hire a ghostwriter to pretty it up.

If you don't agree with the feedback, find a second person to review the book and compare the responses. Then revise accordingly.

Process Component 6: Editing

Now that you've finished your third draft (and possibly a fourth draft, if your reviewer gave you feedback that triggered a revision), you should hire a professional editor.

Your third draft acted as the first part of the editing process, but a seasoned editor will catch all your mistakes and help you with formatting. I have an editor who reviews all of my books. His job is to act as a second pair of eyes on the content and catch the mistakes that I make.

You will want to develop a relationship with an editor as well. You can find one on *Odesk* or *Elance*. When choosing an editor, ask for the following:

- English as their primary language
- Sample editorial work
- A three-page free edit to showcase ability and to get an idea of what level of edits the editor recommends
- Pricing on a proofread, a light edit and a heavy edit

- References from previous clients
- Proof he or she has edited your type of material before (i.e., eBooks, novels, short stories, screenplays, etc.)

Don't hire a brand new editor who doesn't have experience. Make sure your editor is familiar with your field and genre.

You will also want to be clear about what level of edit you expect to receive. The following are descriptions of typical levels of editing:

Proofread – A quick check for grammar, spelling, punctuation and formatting. No rewording whatsoever.

Light edit – Some rewording, only when the text is awkward, plus all the services included in a proofread.

Heavy edit – Rewording throughout the text, including suggestions for changes in content or restructuring of the book, plus all the services provided in a light edit.

Once you get your book off to the editor, you can relax and start thinking about how to promote it.

Process Component 7: Complete a Final Proof

When you get your book back from the editor, you'll want to read through it one last time. Chances are you won't find any mistakes, but even editors miss problems sometimes.

What I like to do is preview it on the medium that most readers will use to access the finished work. So if it's a blog post, then I'll review it on the blog post (instead of the editing console in WordPress.) On the other hand, if it's a Kindle book, I'll download it to two different e-readers (my iPhone and CloudReader) to see how it looks.

When doing a final proof, you should check hyperlinks, look for grammar mistakes and catch other small mistakes. This *isn't* the time to do a major edit. If you start rewriting text, you might disrupt formatting or make more problems. Instead, just make sure your book is the best it can be. Ultimately, the goal of a final proof is to create a polished version that readers will enjoy.

Writing as a Lifelong Habit (or "How to Write 2,000 Words EVERY Day")

Now that you have established a process and a sequence of habits, writing is no longer something you do once in a while. You will establish a permanent habit that will bring you happiness and at least a little bit of income.

While you don't have to write 2,000 words a day, you *do* want to commit to a daily goal that you'll complete every single day.

The key to this commitment is to focus on *developing specific habits and processes* that turn writing into a part of your daily life, just like brushing your teeth or getting good sleep at night. Writing will become a part of your everyday routine, something you always do.

Just like any other habit, writing requires sacrifice and focus. You will need to keep up with these writing habits, especially for the first 30 days as you establish your new writing practice. The longer you continue these specific actions, the more you will settle into a routine that becomes second nature.

I find it helpful to think of myself as a writer—not just as a person who likes to write or hopes to publish a few ebooks. I call myself a writer; I collect writing materials. I deliberately commit my time to my writing habit every day, refusing to let sickness or distractions get in the way. My writing habit is an essential part of my business, but it has also become a part of who I am. *I am a writer.*

You will want to commit to the following mindset and series of habits:

- Label yourself (publicly and privately) as a writer.
- Let important people in your life know about your daily commitment to writing, but don't let any negativity or comments derail you from this goal.
- Schedule your writing time into your daily life as an immovable fixture in your calendar.
- Commit to reasonable writing goals and celebrate each accomplishment.

You don't have to produce masterpieces on your first few attempts. You will improve as you hone your craft. Be careful not to waste your time comparing your first book to bestsellers or literary giants. The only thing you can do is give the best possible effort on your current project and get helpful feedback from others on how to improve on your efforts.

The goal here is to create a lifelong writing habit that brings you joy and a little income on the side. If you've established a writing habit, you have taken the first step towards developing a routine that can bring you a lot of personal and professional success.

Start Writing Today!

You may need to go through this book as a process several times before your writing habit is truly entrenched. I suggest you reread the book, making practical notes as to how you'll implement each of these habits. Then use my 30-Day Habit Challenge (http://www.developgoodhabits.com/30-day-habit-challenge/) to establish specific, actionable goals for every single month:

Stick with it, even if some parts of the program don't feel right at first.

For example, you may want to edit as you write your first draft, but you'll need to force yourself to just write stream-of-consciousness style, refusing to get bogged down in researching facts or editing for grammar. Later, you'll see the value in this, especially when you compare your productivity to previous attempts to write a book.

As you go through the motions the first time through, you'll want to remind yourself of these five key points:

1. It takes repetition for something to become a habit. You have to keep going if you want to establish a writing habit, even if it feels difficult at first.

2. Your writing will improve as your habit becomes more and more established. The best is yet to come!

3. You are forming a new habit that will bring you great joy and satisfaction.

4. You can overcome writer's block by establishing a process for this activity and following it every day.

5. You will continue to improve over time, just as long as you commit to setting a daily word count and learning from each completed project.

Writing is a form of creativity that will enhance your life. Persevere in this and you will reap the rewards tenfold as time passes and your writing habit becomes a part of your everyday life!

Cheers,
S. J. Scott
http://www.DevelopGoodHabits.com

Would You Like to Know More?

The hardest part about starting a habit (like writing) is turning it into a permanent routine. The truth is we often *procrastinate* on major goals because they're paralyzed by uncertainty. This is true even when writing is something we've always wanted to do.

One way to fix this problem is to adopt an "anti-procrastination" mindset. When you know *how* to take action on a consistent basis, you can systematically accomplish any goal. In my book, *23 Anti-Procrastination Habits*, you'll get a series of simple-to-follow routines that can help in your journey towards creating a permanent writing habit.

You can learn more here: http://www.developgoodhabits.com/book-23aph

Thank You

Before you go, I'd like to say "thank you" for purchasing my guide.

I know you could have picked from dozens of books on habit development, but you took a chance with my system.

So a big thanks for ordering this book and reading all the way to the end.

Now I'd like ask for a *small* favor. Could you please take a minute or two and leave a review for this book on Amazon?
http://www.developgoodhabits.com/writing-habit.

This feedback will help me continue to write the kind of books that help you get results. And if you loved it, then please let me know :-)

More Books by S.J. Scott

- *Resolutions That Stick! How 12 Habits Can Transform Your New Year*

- *23 Anti-Procrastination Habits: How to Stop Being Lazy and Get Results in Your Life*

- *Wake Up Successful: How to Increase Your Energy and Achieve Any Goal with a Morning Routine*

- *10,000 Steps Blueprint: The Daily Walking Habit for Healthy Weight Loss and Lifelong Fitness*

- *70 Healthy Habits: How to Eat Better, Feel Great, Get More Energy and Live a Healthy Lifestyle*

About the Author

"Build a Better Life - One Habit at a Time"

Getting more from life doesn't mean following the latest diet craze or motivation program. True success happens when you take action on a daily basis. In other words, it's your habits that help you achieve goals and live the life you've always wanted.

In his books, S.J. provides daily action plans for every area of your life: health, fitness, work and personal relationships. Unlike other personal development guides, his content focuses on taking action. So instead of reading over-hyped strategies that rarely work in the real-world, you'll get information that can be immediately implemented

When not writing, S.J. likes to read, exercise and explore the different parts of the world.

Made in the USA
Lexington, KY
22 July 2014